Stokesay Castle

SHROPSHIRE RECIPES

compiled by
Dorothy Baldock

with paintings by
A. R. Quinton

SALMON

INDEX

Cover pictures: *front:* Ludlow from Whitcliffe
back: River Severn at Bridgnorth

Printed and Published by J. Salmon Ltd., Sevenoaks, England ©

SHROPSHIRE APPLE COBS

12 oz. prepared shortcrust pastry
4 cooking apples
6 heaped teaspoons thick honey
½ oz. butter, softened
½ to 1 teaspoon mixed spice
A little milk or beaten egg to glaze
20 cloves to decorate

This delicious apple pudding is a Shropshire variation of the ever-popular apple dumpling.

Set oven to 350°F or Mark 4. Roll out the pastry on a lightly floured surface and cut four circles, slightly larger than the base of each apple, from just under one half of the pastry. Set these on a greased baking sheet. Peel and core the apples and place on the pastry circles. Mix together the honey and butter and use to fill the apples, then sprinkle over a little spice. Roll out the remainder of the pastry, divide into four circles and place these over the apples as 'lids' and smooth down. Turn up the edges of the base circles, dampen and seal well with the lids, fluting slightly to form a little frill. Brush with milk or beaten egg to glaze and bake for 20 to 30 minutes or until golden. Just before serving, push five cloves into the top of each Cob to form a 'crown'. Serve hot, with custard or thick cream.

On the Teme

GRAYLING IN BEER

4 grayling, gutted, scaled and
well washed
1 pint beer
2 level teaspoons grated horseradish
1 teaspoon grated lemon rind
Salt
Black pepper
Sprigs of fresh thyme
¾ oz. butter
Lemon slices and thyme sprigs
for garnish

The grayling is a silvery fish, a relation of
the salmon and trout, found in swift-
flowing rivers. Its flesh is said to have the
scent of thyme.

Using a sharp knife, make three or four scores on each side of the fish. Place in a large, deep frying pan and pour on the beer. Sprinkle with the horseradish and lemon rind and season well. Top with thyme sprigs. Bring to the boil, cover and simmer until the fish is tender – about 15 minutes. Very carefully remove the fish from the cooking liquid, drain and place on a warm serving dish. Strain the cooking liquid and measure ¼-pint into a saucepan. Add the butter, heat through and pour the sauce over the fish. Serve garnished with lemon slices and thyme sprigs and accompanied by creamed horseradish sauce and brown bread and butter. Serves 4.

SHROPSHIRE PEA SOUP

2 oz. butter
1 small onion, peeled and chopped
2 lb. fresh peas, shelled
¼ teaspoon sugar
1 sprig fresh mint
2 sprigs fresh parsley
Salt
Black pepper
2 pints chicken stock
2 egg yolks
5 fl. oz. double cream
4 sprigs of fresh mint for garnish

Melt the butter in a large saucepan, add the onion and cook for 5 minutes until soft, but not browned. Add the peas, sugar, herbs and seasoning. Then add the stock and bring to the boil. Simmer for 30-40 minutes, allow to cool a little then put through a sieve or purée in a liquidiser. Return to a clean saucepan and heat through. Beat the egg yolks and cream together and add to the soup. Heat gently, stirring, but do not allow the soup to boil or it will curdle. Pour into 4 soup bowls and serve garnished with mint sprigs.

A substantial soup of fresh peas with onions, mint, parsley and double cream.

LAMBING CAKE

4 oz. margarine or butter
4 oz. sugar
2 eggs, beaten
8 oz. self-raising flour
2 level teaspoons mixed spice
½ teaspoon ground cinnamon
½ teaspoon ground ginger
Salt
2 oz. sultanas or currants
3 fl. oz. milk and water, equally mixed

Set oven to 325°F or Mark 3. Cream the fat and sugar together in a bowl until light and fluffy, then beat in the eggs, a little at a time. Sift together the flour, spices and salt and fold into the mixture, then add the fruit and sufficient liquid to produce a soft, dropping consistency. Turn the mixture into a greased and base-lined 2 lb. loaf tin and smooth the top. Bake for 20 minutes, then reduce the oven temperature to 300°F or Mark 2 for a further 40-50 minutes, covering the top with a piece of kitchen foil if it appears to be browning too quickly. Cool in the tin for 5 minutes, then turn out on to a wire rack. Serve sliced, plain or with butter.

A teabread containing ginger, cinnamon and dried fruit. A 'stand by' snack during lambing time.

*H*ARE *P*IE

2 to 3 tablespoons flour
1 level teaspoon grated nutmeg
½ level teaspoon dry mustard powder
Salt and black pepper
2 to 2½ lbs. hare meat, wiped and cubed
3 rashers streaky bacon, de-rinded and chopped
2 oz. butter
2 onions or 6 shallots, peeled and chopped
A bouquet garni
1 teaspoon grated lemon rind
¾ pint vegetable stock
4 tablespoons port
2 teaspoons lemon juice
4 mushrooms, wiped and sliced
8 oz. prepared shortcrust or puff pastry
Beaten egg to glaze

Set oven to 325°F or Mark 3. Mix together the flour, nutmeg, mustard and seasoning, toss the hare meat and bacon in this and then place it in an ovenproof casserole dish. Melt the butter in a frying pan and lightly fry the onion or shallots for one minute, then add to the casserole with the *bouquet garni* and lemon rind. Pour over the stock, bring to the boil, cover and cook for 2 to 3 hours or until the meat is tender. Allow to cool, discard the herbs, then add the port, lemon juice and mushrooms and adjust the seasoning if necessary. Turn into a 2½ to 3 pint pie dish with a pie funnel in the centre. Set oven to 375°F or Mark 5. Roll out the pastry on a lightly floured surface and use to cover the pie, trimming the edges neatly. Decorate with leaves cut from the pastry trimmings and brush with beaten egg to glaze. Bake for 30 to 40 minutes, or until the pastry is golden brown. Serve with creamed potatoes and a green vegetable and accompanied by redcurrant or crab apple jelly. Serves 4 to 6.

This well-flavoured game pie, which can be topped either with shortcrust or puff pastry, whichever is preferred, is traditionally served with redcurrant or crab apple jelly. However, if desired, Hare Pie can also be served with the additional accompaniment of English veal forcemeat balls.

Old houses at Frankwell

SHREWSBURY SAUCE

2 oz. butter
1 carrot, peeled and chopped
2 shallots, peeled and chopped
1 stick of celery, wiped, trimmed and chopped
2 mushrooms, wiped and sliced
2 level tablespoons flour mixed with a pinch each of mustard powder and ground nutmeg
Salt and black pepper
1 pint lamb stock
3 sprigs parsley, 1 sprig thyme, 1 small sprig rosemary and a 'curl' of lemon rind, tied together with a piece of kitchen string
¼ pint port, cheapest brand
2 teaspoons lemon juice
4 heaped tablespoons redcurrant jelly

Melt the butter in a saucepan and lightly fry the vegetables until the butter is absorbed. Stir in the flour and seasoning and cook, stirring, for 2 minutes. Whisk in the stock, then add the *bouquet garni*. Bring to the boil, then cover and simmer for 30 to 40 minutes. Add the port and lemon juice and simmer for a further 10 to 15 minutes. Discard the *bouquet garni* and sieve the sauce. Just before serving, stir in the redcurrant jelly and heat through thoroughly. Serve in a sauce boat.

A rich variant of Redcurrant Sauce, this is a perfect 'special occasion' accompaniment to new season roast lamb. Shrewsbury Sauce is also excellent with roast venison.

SOUL CAKES

6 oz. butter, softened
6 oz. caster sugar
3 egg yolks
1 lb. flour
Pinch of salt
1 teaspoon allspice or mixed spice
3 oz. currants
A little warm milk

On All Souls' Day, 2nd November, the dead are remembered and children would go 'a-souling'. Singing "A soul-cake, a soul-cake, please, good missus, a soul-cake. One for Peter, two for Paul, three for Him who saved us all." They would receive, in return, a cake marked with a cross.

Set oven to 350°F or Mark 4. Cream the butter and sugar together in a bowl until fluffy, then beat in the egg yolks. Sift together the flour, salt and spice and fold into the egg mixture with the currants, adding sufficient milk to form a soft dough. Divide into pieces and form into flat cakes, marking each with a cross. Place on a greased baking sheet and bake for 20 minutes or until golden. If desired, a few threads of saffron can be soaked in the warm milk, straining it before use.

Towards the Clee Hills from Ludlow

SHROPSHIRE FRIED CAKES

8 oz. self-raising flour
2 oz. butter
2 oz. sugar
A little milk
Lard, butter or cooking oil for frying

Sift the flour into a bowl and rub in the butter until the mixture resembles fine breadcrumbs. Stir in the sugar, then add sufficient milk to make a firm dough. Turn out on to a lightly floured surface and roll out to ½ inch thick and cut into rounds. Melt the lard, butter or cooking oil in a frying pan and, when hot, add the cakes. Cook on one side until well risen on top and golden brown underneath, then turn over and cook on the other side. Drain on kitchen paper and eat whilst still warm.

Traditionally these cakes were fried in bacon fat and eaten as a harvest snack by farm workers. Today they can be enjoyed as a breakfast dish or a snack at any time, either on their own or with fried bacon rashers.

LEEK AND CABBAGE SOUP

2 pints chicken stock
6 leeks, washed, trimmed and cut into ½ inch rings
2 lb. cabbage, washed, trimmed of outer leaves and stalks and chopped into shreds
1 large onion, peeled and finely sliced
6 sprigs of fresh parsley, tied together with kitchen string
Salt
Black pepper
Grated cheese or chopped fresh parsley for garnish

Bring the stock to the boil in a large saucepan. Add the leeks, cabbage, onion and parsley and bring back to the boil. Cover and simmer for 40-50 minutes, stirring occasionally. Season to taste and remove the parsley sprigs. Spoon into four soup bowls, dividing the vegetables and serve garnished with grated cheese or chopped parsley, as preferred and accompanied by crusty granary bread.

A recipe which is also known as Miners' Soup.

Kidney and Sausage Casserole

1 oz. butter
2 onions, peeled and sliced
1 to 2 tablespoons flour, seasoned with a pinch of dry mustard
1 lb. pork sausages
2 to 3 lambs' kidneys, wiped, cored and sliced
4 sprigs parsley, 2 sprigs thyme and 2 sage leaves tied together with a piece of kitchen string
Salt and black pepper
1 to 2 pints pork stock
A little fresh chopped parsley for garnish

An economical farmhouse recipe.

Set oven to 300°F or Mark 2. Melt the butter in a frying pan and lightly fry the onion until soft, but still transparent, then stir in the seasoned flour. Prick the sausages lightly with a fork and place in an ovenproof casserole with the kidneys. Add the herbs and seasoning. Pour the stock over the onion and flour mixture and bring to the boil, stirring, then pour sufficient into the casserole to cover the contents. Cover and cook for about 5 hours. Discard the herbs and allow to cool overnight. Next day, set oven to 325°F or Mark 3 and cook the casserole for 30 to 40 minutes until completely heated through, topping up the gravy, if necessary. Sprinkle with chopped parsley and serve with mashed potatoes, carrots and a green vegetable. Serves 4.

WELSH MUTTON PIES

PASTRY
8 oz. lard
1 lb. flour
1 teaspoon salt
¼ pint milk and water, equally mixed

FILLING
1 lb. lamb, finely minced
8 oz. currants
4 oz. brown sugar
Salt and black pepper
Milk or beaten egg for glazing

To make the raised pie pastry; in a bowl, rub 2 oz. lard into the flour, then stir in the salt. Put the remainder of the lard and the milk and water into a saucepan and bring to the boil. Make a well in the flour mixture, stir in the boiling liquid and combine well with a wooden spoon until the mixture leaves the sides of the bowl. Allow to cool a little, then turn out on to a lightly floured surface and knead until smooth and pliable and still warm. Divide into 8 pieces and roll out to about ½ inch thick. Using a lightly greased 3½ inch individual soufflé dish as a mould, form each piece of pastry into a pie shape, trimming the tops neatly and reserving the trimmings. Divide the lamb, currants and sugar between the pies, layering them and seasoning well between each layer. Roll out the trimmings and cut out 8 lids. Place on the pies, crimping the edges and sealing well with a little water. Make a steam hole in the centre of each pie and brush with milk or beaten egg to glaze. Place on a lightly greased baking sheet and allow to stand for 10 minutes to 'firm up'. Set oven to 375°F or Mark 5 and bake the pies for 30-35 minutes or until crisp and golden.

Although these pies are traditionally made with raised pie pastry, they can be made with puff pastry; in which case they are baked in lightly greased patty tins. Also known as Katt Pies, they were traditionally eaten at the Mop or Hiring Fairs held in the autumn, when farm workers and house servants would hire themselves out for the coming year.

Clun Castle

SAVOURY VEAL

1 lb. English veal fillet, wiped and trimmed
1 oz. flour
½ teaspoon fresh, finely chopped sage
½ teaspoon fresh, finely chopped marjoram
Salt and white pepper
1 to 1½ pints chicken or vegetable stock
1 oz. butter, softened
Lemon slices and parsley sprigs for garnish

This is the traditional Shrewsbury way of cooking fillet of veal.

Scald a pudding cloth in boiling water, wring out well and dust with half the flour, then sprinkle over the herbs and seasoning. Roll the fillet in the cloth and tie securely with string. In a large saucepan, bring the stock to the boil, then add the fillet and poach over gentle heat for 1 to 1½ hours or until tender. Set oven to 450°F or Mark 8. Reserving the poaching liquid, carefully lift the fillet from the saucepan and remove the cloth. Smooth over the butter and dust with the remaining flour, to which a little seasoning has been added. Place in a roasting tin and cook for 10 to 15 minutes until browned. Use the reserved liquid as a basis for a rich white sauce. Garnish with lemon slices and parsley sprigs and serve with creamed potatoes, carrots and a green vegetable, with the sauce. Serves 4.

CARAWAY SODA BREAD

1 lb. flour
1 teaspoon bicarbonate of soda
1 teaspoon sugar
1 teaspoon salt
12 fl. oz. sour milk or buttermilk
Caraway seeds

A variation of the ubiquitous Soda Bread, flavoured with caraway seeds.

Set oven to 450°F or Mark 8. Grease a 7 inch square shallow baking tin and sprinkle liberally with caraway seeds. Sieve the dry ingredients together into a bowl. Make a well in the centre and pour in most of the milk. Mix to a soft but not sticky dough, adding more milk if necessary. Turn out on to a lightly floured surface and knead gently for about half a minute. Put into the tin, spread out and sprinkle with more caraway seeds. Make several diagonal cuts across the top. Bake for 15 minutes then reduce heat to 400°F or Mark 6 and bake for about a further 30 minutes; the base of the bread should sound hollow when tapped. Cover with kitchen foil if the top seems to be browning too quickly. Cut into slices and butter.

Sentinels of the Border

WELSH BORDER TART

1 oz. butter
4 oz. light brown sugar
4 oz. raisins
4 oz. sultanas
1 teaspoon lemon juice or
a few drops of vanilla essence
3 eggs, separated
3 oz. caster sugar
8 oz. prepared shortcrust pastry

This meringue-topped lemon dessert
can be served hot or cold.

In a saucepan, melt the butter and allow it to cool slightly, then stir in the brown sugar, fruit and lemon juice or vanilla essence. Combine well together, then add the egg yolks. Set oven to 350°F or Mark 4. Roll out the pastry on a lightly floured surface and use to line a well greased 8 inch flan case, trimming the edges neatly. Spoon in the filling and smooth the top, then bake for 30 minutes. Remove from the oven. Whisk the egg whites until they stand up in soft peaks, then fold in the caster sugar with a metal spoon. Reduce the oven temperature to 300°F or Mark 2. Pile or pipe the meringue on top of the filling and bake for 10-15 minutes, or until the meringue is a soft golden-brown. Serve hot or cold, accompanied by single cream. Serves 4 to 6.

*B*LACKBERRY *F*LUMMERY

1 lb. fresh blackberries, washed and hulled
½ pint water
1 oz. butter
1 oz. flour
4 oz. sugar
1 egg, separated
1 teaspoon lemon juice
Cream to decorate

Flummeries – a form of blancmange – date back to medieval times, but were a particularly popular dessert in Tudor days. Other soft fruits, such as raspberries, blackcurrants, etcetera can be used in place of blackberries.

Cook the blackberries in a little water until soft, then sieve to produce a smooth purée. Allow to cool. Heat the ½ pint of water and the butter together in a saucepan until hot but not boiling, then remove from the heat. Mix the flour and sugar together and stir in, beating until smooth. Whisk the egg yolk into the mixture, return to the heat and cook, stirring, for 5 minutes; do not allow to boil. Stir the lemon juice into the blackberry purée and add to the mixture. Allow to cool a little. Whisk the egg white until it stands up in soft peaks and fold into the blackberry mixture. Turn into a serving dish and chill well. Whip the cream until it stands up in soft peaks and pipe on to the flummery to decorate. Serve with boudoir or cat's tongue biscuits. Serves 4.

SHEARING CAKE

1 lb. flour
2 teaspoons baking powder
Pinch of salt
½ teaspoon ground nutmeg
½ teaspoon ground ginger
8 oz. butter, softened
8 oz. soft brown sugar
1 tablespoon caraway seeds
The rind of a lemon
1 dessertspoon of lemon juice
2 tablespoons clear honey, slightly warmed
½ pint buttermilk
2 eggs, beaten

This substantial cake was traditionally served at sheep-shearing time – a social as well as a working occasion.

Set oven to 350°F or Mark 4. Sift together the flour, baking powder, salt and spices into a bowl, rub in the butter until the mixture resembles fine breadcrumbs, then add the sugar, caraway seeds and lemon rind. Mix together the lemon juice and honey and stir into the mixture. Lightly combine together the milk and eggs and beat into mixture. Turn into a greased and base lined 9 inch round cake tin, smooth over the top and bake for 30 minutes. Reduce the temperature to 300°F or Mark 2 and bake for a further 1½ to 2 hours, covering the top with a piece of kitchen foil if it appears to be browning too quickly. Cool in the tin for 10 minutes, then turn out on to a wire rack.

SHROPSHIRE FIDGET PIE

3 medium potatoes, peeled and finely sliced
2 onions, peeled and sliced
2 cooking apples, peeled, cored and sliced
3 rashers sweetcure gammon, de-rinded and cut into strips
1½ oz. butter
1 dessertspoon brown sugar
Salt and black pepper
½ teaspoon ground nutmeg
¼ pint pork or vegetable stock
8 oz. prepared shortcrust pastry
Milk or beaten egg to glaze

The name of this pie is said to come from the fact that it was originally 'fitched' or five-sided in shape.

Set oven to 350°F or Mark 4. Lightly fry the sliced potatoes, onions and apples in the butter until just golden. Remove with a slotted spoon and keep warm. Place the gammon in the pan and fry lightly in the remaining fat. Layer the gammon and the potatoes, onions and apples in a 1½-2 pint pie dish, seasoning with sugar, salt, pepper and nutmeg. Pour on the stock. On a lightly floured surface roll out the pastry and cover the pie, trimming the edges. Make a steam hole and decorate with the trimmings. Brush with milk or egg. Bake for 30 minutes, then reduce the oven to 325°F or Mark 3 for a further 10-15 minutes or until the pie is golden brown. Traditionally this pie is not served with vegetables, but carrots or cabbage can be served if desired. Serves 4 to 6.

Bridgnorth from the Severn

HEART AND KIDNEY PUDDING

3 lamb's hearts, washed and trimmed
4 lamb's kidneys, washed and the cores removed
1 small onion, peeled and chopped
½ lb. prepared suet pastry
1 teaspoon chopped mixed herbs
Salt
Black pepper
½ pint lamb stock

Chop the hearts and kidneys into cubes and dust with a little seasoned flour. Mix with the onion. Roll out the pastry on a lightly floured surface and use two-thirds to line a well greased 2 pint pudding basin. Put the heart, kidney and onion into the basin and sprinkle with the herbs. Season and pour in the stock. Roll out the remaining pastry and use as a lid, sealing the edges well. Cover with greased greaseproof paper and cover and seal with kitchen foil. Steam for 3-3½ hours. Turn out of the basin and serve with boiled potatoes, carrots and a green vegetable. Serves 4.

This pudding can also be made using pig's hearts and kidneys – in which case the mixed herbs should be replaced by a ¼ teaspoon of chopped sage.

GAME SOUP

2 Pheasant carcasses
2 Partridge carcasses
1 large onion, peeled and diced
2 carrots, scraped and diced
2 strips of celery, washed and diced
¼ lb lean bacon rashers, de-rinded and diced
2 oz. butter
1 tablespoon cooking oil
A bouquet garni
Salt and black pepper
1 small glass of port
1 tablespoon redcurrant jelly

This luxury soup is a convenient way to use up the left-over carcasses of any species of game birds. The mixture of birds will depend upon availability.

If the carcasses are raw, having been jointed and the breasts removed for a casserole, melt the butter with the oil in a pan and fry all over until brown. If, however, the carcasses are the remains of roasted birds then the frying is unnecessary. Remove from the pan, if fried, put into a large saucepan, cover with water and bring to the boil. Add the *bouquet garni*, cover with a lid and simmer for 2 hours. Meanwhile, fry the bacon and vegetables until softened but not brown. Remove the carcasses and the *bouquet garni* from the stock, add the bacon and vegetables, season to taste and simmer for a further 30 minutes until the vegetables are tender. Check the seasoning, stir in the port and redcurrant jelly and serve piping hot with granary rolls. Serves 4.

Shrewsbury Castle

Shrewsbury Biscuits

4 oz. butter
5 oz. caster sugar
2 egg yolks
8 oz. flour
Finely grated rind of a lemon

Set oven to 350°F or Mark 4. Cream the butter and sugar together in a bowl until light and fluffy, then beat in the egg yolks. Add the flour and the lemon rind and mix, forming a fairly firm dough. Turn out on to a lightly floured surface, knead lightly for 1 minute, then roll out to about ¼ inch thick. Using a fluted 2½ inch cutter, cut into rounds and place on a lightly greased baking sheet. Bake for 12-15 minutes until golden and firm to the touch. Cool on a wire rack. Makes about 20 biscuits.

Sometimes known as Shrewsbury Cakes or Shrewsbury Easter Biscuits, they have been made since the 16th century and traditionally were offered to notable visitors to Shrewsbury.

There are other traditional flavour variations, including mixed spice, caraway seeds, rose-water and currants.

SHROPSHIRE PIE

2 oz. flour
½ level teaspoon mustard powder
½ level teaspoon ground nutmeg
Salt and black pepper
6 to 8 rabbit joints, wiped
3 rashers streaky bacon, rinds removed and cut into strips
1 onion, peeled and sliced
1 small cooking apple, peeled, cored and sliced
1 dessertspoon of currants, if desired
1 bayleaf
A curl of lemon rind

4 oz. fresh white breadcrumbs
1 oz. shredded suet
2 tablespoons fresh chopped parsley
½ teaspoon fresh chopped thyme
1 teaspoon grated lemon rind
Salt and black pepper
Pinch ground nutmeg
1 egg yolk
1 to 2 teaspoons lemon juice
½ pint chicken stock
¼ pint red wine
8 oz. prepared puff pastry
Beaten egg to glaze

This luxury rabbit pie dates from the 18th century; the original recipe also contained oysters and artichoke bottoms.

Mix together the flour, mustard, nutmeg and seasoning, coat the rabbit joints and place in a 2 to 2½ pint pie dish. Sprinkle over the bacon, onion and apple and currants, if desired, then add the bayleaf and curl of lemon rind. Mix together the breadcrumbs, suet, thyme, lemon rind, seasoning, nutmeg and half of the parsley and bind with the egg yolk and lemon juice. If the mixture is too dry, add a little stock. Form into balls and place among the rabbit joints. Sprinkle over the remaining parsley. Mix together the red wine and stock and pour over, half filling the pie dish. Reserve any excess liquid. Set oven to 425°F or Mark 7. Roll out the pastry on a lightly floured surface and use to cover the pie, trimming the edges neatly and making a steam hole in the centre. Decorate with leaves cut from the trimmings and glaze with beaten egg. Bake for 15 to 20 minutes, then reduce the oven temperature to 350°F or Mark 4 and bake for a further 1 to 1½ hours until golden, covering with a piece of kitchen foil if the pastry appears to be browning too quickly. Before serving, heat any remaining liquid and pour into the pie through the steam hole. Serve with creamed or boiled potatoes, grilled mushrooms, carrots and a green vegetable. Serves 4 to 6.

Chicken can be substituted for rabbit in this recipe. In which case, white wine should replace the red and, at the end of the baking time, a little warmed double cream should be poured into the pie through the steam hole before serving. This makes a delicious pie, though, of course, no longer a traditional Shropshire one.

LOIN OF PORK AND CABBAGE CAKE

3-3½ lb. loin of pork, chined and scored
2 tablespoons flour
Salt
1 tablespoon cooking oil
½ pint pork stock
2 lb. white cabbage, washed, trimmed and finely shredded
1 oz. butter
1 onion, peeled and chopped
2 oz. sultanas, optional
1 tablespoon fresh chopped parsley
Salt and black pepper
2 medium cooking apples, peeled, cored and thickly sliced
Fresh chopped parsley for garnish

Set oven to 400°F or Mark 6. Rub the pork with the flour, then sprinkle with the salt. Heat the oil in a roasting tin, then add the pork and roast for 1-1½ hours, basting several times during the cooking period. Meanwhile, blanch the cabbage in boiling water for 3 minutes, then drain well. Melt the butter in a flame-proof casserole or skillet, add the onion and cook until soft but not brown. Remove from the casserole and stir into the cabbage, add the sultanas, if desired and the parsley and seasoning. Place the apples in a layer in the base of the casserole, place the cabbage mixture on top and press down well – a potato masher is ideal. Put on the lid and cook gently on the top of the stove for 10 minutes then transfer to the oven and cook with the pork for 40 minutes. Place the pork on a warm serving dish and keep hot. Drain all but 1 tablespoon of fat from the roasting tin and stir 1 tablespoon of flour into the tin. Stir in the stock and bring to the boil, stirring all the time, season and pour into a sauceboat. Turn the cabbage cake out on to a warm serving dish and garnish with parsley. Serve with the pork, accompanied by roast potatoes and the gravy. Serves 4 to 6.

This is a dish which was traditionally served in the Welsh Marches at pig-killing time, which was an occasion for celebration, when the family pig was despatched to produce hams, bacon, sausages, black puddings, pies and much more to carry on through the ensuing months.

The Feathers, Ludlow

Welsh Cakes

8 oz. self-raising flour
Salt
2 oz. butter
2 oz. lard
3 oz. sugar
3 oz. sultanas or currants
1 egg, beaten
A little milk

Sift together the flour and salt into a bowl, then rub in the fats until the mixture resembles fine breadcrumbs. Stir in the sugar and fruit, then add the egg, mixing to form a firm dough, adding a little milk if necessary. Roll out on to a lightly floured surface to about ¼ inch thick, then cut into 3 inch rounds. Lightly grease a hot griddle or frying pan and cook the cakes, turning once, until golden brown. Serve hot, with butter. Makes 12 to 14 cakes.

Popular in the Welsh Border counties, these little cakes, originally baked on a heated 'bakestone' were often served to travellers on their arrival at an inn.

WIMBERRY PIE

12 oz. shortcrust pastry
1½ lb. wimberries, rinsed and
well drained
3 oz. caster sugar or more if preferred
Milk to glaze and
extra caster sugar for sprinkling

Set oven to 400°F or Mark 6. Roll out the pastry on a lightly floured surface and use half to line an 8 inch pie plate. Fill the pie with the wimberries and sprinkle over the 3 oz. sugar. Cover with the remaining pastry, seal the edges, trim and decorate as preferred and make a steam hole in the centre. Brush with milk and sprinkle with caster sugar. Place on a baking sheet and bake for 30 minutes then reduce heat to 350°F or Mark 4 and cook for a further 15 minutes. Serve hot or cold with double cream. Serves 4 to 6.

Wimberries are small, dark mauve berries which grow wild on the Shropshire hills.

In Border Country

Sir Watkin William Wynne's Pudding

5 oz. fresh white breadcrumbs
4 oz. sugar
3 oz. shredded suet
2 eggs, separated
Grated rind and juice of a lemon
1 teaspoon brandy

BRANDY SAUCE
2 eggs
1 oz. sugar
2 tablespoons brandy
1 tablespoon hot water

This hunting pudding is named after a Welsh Border Squire who hunted enthusiastically in the Marches.

Mix the breadcrumbs, sugar and suet together in a bowl, then stir in the egg yolks with the lemon rind and juice and brandy and combine well. Whisk the egg whites until they stand up in soft peaks, then fold into the mixture. Turn into a well buttered 1½-2 pint pudding basin and cover with buttered greaseproof paper and seal with kitchen foil. Place in a saucepan, add sufficient boiling water to come halfway up the basin and steam for 2 hours, topping up the water as necessary. Turn out on to a warm serving dish and serve with Brandy Sauce, custard or cream. Serves 4 to 6.

BRANDY SAUCE: Place all the ingredients in a bowl suspended over a saucepan of hot water and whisk until thick and creamy.

SHROPSHIRE SUMMER SOUP

1 oz. butter
2 onions, peeled and finely chopped
1 large potato, peeled and diced
½ medium cucumber, peeled and cubed
1 medium lettuce, washed, trimmed and cut into ½ inch strips
4 oz. fresh spinach, washed, trimmed and chopped
1 oz. fresh peas, weighed after shucking
A bouquet garni with a curl of lemon rind
1¾ to 2 pints chicken or vegetable stock
1 teaspoon lemon juice
Salt and white pepper
½ pint double cream
Fresh peas, cooked and cooled, fresh chopped mint and fresh chopped parsley, for garnish

A chilled soup made with the freshest of summer vegetables.

Melt the butter in a large saucepan and lightly cook the onion until soft, but still transparent. Add the remainder of the vegetables, herbs and lemon rind, then pour over the stock and lemon juice and season. Bring to the boil, then reduce the heat and simmer, covered, for 30 to 40 minutes. Remove the *bouquet garni* and allow the soup to cool completely. Sieve or liquidize and adjust the seasoning, if necessary. Reserving two tablespoons of cream, stir the remainder into the soup and chill for *at least* 1 hour before serving. Pour into bowls and garnish each with a swirl of cream, a few peas and a sprinkling of mint and parsley. Serve with rolls or crusty bread. Serves 4 to 6.

PIGEON CASSEROLE

3 pigeons plucked, drawn and jointed
2 to 3 tablespoons cooking oil
4 oz. smoked bacon rashers, de-rinded and diced
1 large onion, peeled and sliced
2 carrots, scraped and diced
3 tablespoons flour
1 pint chicken stock
¼ pint dry white wine
Salt and black pepper

Set oven to 325°F or Mark 3. Fry the pigeons in the oil for about 5 minutes until brown all over. Remove from the pan and put into a lidded casserole dish. Fry the bacon, onion and carrots until softened but not brown and add to the casserole. Stir the flour into the remaining oil, remove the pan from the heat and mix in the stock and the wine. Pour over the pigeon joints, season well, cover and cook for about 1½ hours. Serve with mashed potatoes, boiled parsnips and a green vegetable. Serves 4.

Keeping down the pigeon population is a continuing battle for countrymen. This recipe contributes to that end.

BOILED SHOULDER OF LAMB *with bacon stuffing*

BACON STUFFING
2 oz. streaky bacon, finely chopped
4 shallots, peeled, and finely chopped
1 oz. shredded suet
2 oz. fresh white breadcrumbs
1 heaped tablespoon chopped parsley
1 teaspoon grated lemon rind
½ teaspoon grated nutmeg
Salt and black pepper
1 egg, beaten

2 to 2½ lb. boned-out shoulder of lamb,
wiped and trimmed
4 back bacon rashers, de-rinded
2 onions, peeled and sliced
2 sticks celery, wiped and chopped
A bouquet garni
1 to 2 pints lamb stock
Salt and black pepper
Sprigs of mint for garnish

Mix all the Bacon Stuffing ingredients together in a bowl, bind with the beaten egg and use to stuff the boned-out shoulder of lamb. Sew up the joint securely. Lay two bacon rashers on the base of a large saucepan, place the joint on top, then top with the remaining two rashers. Add the onions, celery and herbs, pour in the stock and bring to the boil and then skim. Cover and simmer until the joint is tender (allowing 20 minutes for each pound of stuffed weight, plus an extra 20 minutes). Remove the joint from the saucepan, drain very well and keep warm on a serving dish. Strain the stock, skimming off any fat, then bring it to the boil, thickening with a little seasoned flour, if desired. Serve the shoulder of lamb garnished with fresh mint and accompanied by green peas and boiled or creamed potatoes, with the stock served separately in a gravy boat. Serves 4 to 6.

This summertime farmhouse dish was traditionally accompanied by Sorrel Sauce. Nowadays, if desired, a Cucumber Sauce is a more usual alternative.

CUCUMBER SAUCE: ½ oz. butter; 1 small shallot, peeled and chopped; ½-¾ large cucumber, peeled, de-seeded and chopped; ½ pint prepared white sauce; salt and white pepper. Melt the butter, fry the shallot until soft then add the cucumber and fry until soft but not brown. Add the cucumber mixture to the white sauce in a pan and simmer, stirring, for 10 minutes. Liquidise, return to a clean pan, season and heat thoroughly. Serve hot.

Shrewsbury Abbey

Apple Cake

3 cooking apples, peeled, cored and sliced
5 oz. margarine
5 oz. brown sugar
2 eggs, beaten
8 oz. flour
½ teaspoon cinnamon
½ teaspoon bicarbonate of soda
salt
2 oz. sultanas
2 oz. glacé cherries, halved
2 oz. chopped walnuts
Grated rind of half a lemon

A spicy cake which contains glacé cherries and nuts, the apple first being cooked to a pulp. This makes the cake very moist and hence a good 'keeper'.

Cook the apples with a little water until soft, then sieve to produce a smooth purée; there should be 4-5 oz. Allow to cool. Set oven to 350°F or Mark 4. Cream the margarine and sugar together in a bowl until fluffy, then beat in the eggs, a little at a time. Sift together the flour, spices, bicarbonate of soda and salt and stir into the mixture. Add the fruit and chopped nuts. Mix the lemon rind with the apple purée and fold into the mixture. Turn into a greased and baselined 7 inch cake tin and smooth the top. If so desired, a dessertspoon of demerara or granulated sugar can be sprinkled over the cake to give a crunchy topping. Bake for 45 minutes or until golden brown and springy to the touch. Cool in the tin for 5 minutes, then turn out on to a wire rack.

LAMB IN CREAM SAUCE

4 large lamb chops, wiped and trimmed
1 oz. butter
2 onions, peeled and sliced
2 tablespoons flour
8 fl. oz. lamb stock
4 fl. oz. single cream
Salt and black pepper
1 dessertspoon fresh chopped herbs –
parsley, thyme, rosemary, etc.
Parsley sprigs to garnish

Dust the chops with a little seasoned flour and fry in the butter on both sides to seal. Remove with a slotted spoon and keep warm. Fry the onion in the remaining fat until lightly golden, then stir in the flour. Add the stock, a little at a time, stirring between each addition, and bring to the boil. Reduce the heat and stir in the cream, seasoning and herbs. Add the chops, cover and simmer for 25-30 minutes. Serve garnished with parsley sprigs and accompanied by creamed potatoes, peas and carrots. Serves 4.

A country house recipe for lamb chops served in a herb-flavoured cream sauce.

Ludlow Castle from the Meadows

Shropshire Faggots

2 onions, peeled
1 lb. pig's liver
3 oz. mashed potato or white breadcrumbs
A scant ½ pint of pork stock
½ teaspoon fresh, finely chopped sage
1 teaspoon fresh, finely chopped parsley
Salt and black pepper
1 oz. melted butter

Nicknamed Savoury Duck or Poor Man's Goose, Faggots have always been a popular item in pork butchers' shops. Traditionally each faggot should be wrapped in a square of prepared pig's caul or veil, but they can be prepared without this, although they will not hold their shape quite as well during cooking.

Boil the onions in water for 15 minutes. Drain well and allow to cool. Set oven to 425°F or Mark 7. Coarsely mince the onions and liver together and stir in the mashed potato or breadcrumbs. NOTE: if using breadcrumbs, moisten with 2 to 3 tablespoons of hot stock before using. Add herbs, seasoning and melted butter and combine well. Using well floured hands, form the mixture into squares or balls and pack into a well greased baking tin. Thicken the remaining stock and sprinkle over, taking care not to drown the faggots. Cover with a piece of kitchen foil and bake for 30 to 40 minutes, removing the foil for the last 10 to 15 minutes of cooking to brown the faggots. Serve with mashed potatoes and carrots, accompanied by pease pudding and a rich, thickened gravy. Serves 4.

SHROPSHIRE SPECIAL CAKES

4 oz. ground rice
4 oz. flour
Pinch of caraway seeds
4 oz. butter
4 oz. sugar
2 eggs, beaten

Set oven to 375°F or Mark 5. Sift the ground rice and flour together into a bowl, then stir in the caraway seeds. Cream the butter and sugar together until light and fluffy, then combine with the flour mixture. Add the eggs, a little at a time, to form a firm dough. Knead lightly, then turn out on to a lightly floured surface. Roll out to about ¼ inch thickness, using a well floured rolling pin and cut into rounds with a 3-4 inch cutter. Place on a well greased baking sheet and bake for 15 minutes, or until lightly golden.

Like Soul Cakes, these were eaten on All Souls' Day – 2nd November – in memory of the departed. In the Welsh Border counties, children would go 'a-souling'– singing from house to house – and would be given cakes that were traditionally marked with a cross.

Salmon Pie

1 oz. butter
1 large onion, peeled and finely chopped
1 pint prepared white sauce, made with full-cream milk, and quite thick in consistency
2 teaspoons lemon juice
Salt and white pepper
3 tablespoons double cream
1 lb. cooked, flaked salmon
1 oz. lightly toasted breadcrumbs
1 teaspoon fresh, chopped parsley
¼ teaspoon fresh, chopped thyme
8 oz. prepared puff pastry
Beaten egg to glaze

A delicious pie filled with salmon and a creamy onion sauce.

Melt the butter in a pan and cook the onion until soft and transparent, then stir into the white sauce with the lemon juice and seasoning. Heat through, stirring all the time, then add the cream. Allow to cool slightly. Place a layer of salmon over the base of a 2 to 3 pint pie dish, then spoon over a layer of sauce. Continue in this way, finishing with a layer of sauce. Mix together the breadcrumbs and herbs and sprinkle over. Set oven to 450°F or Mark 8. Roll out the pastry on a lightly floured surface and cover the pie, trimming the edges; make a steam-hole. Decorate with trimmings and glaze with beaten egg. Bake for 10 to 15 minutes, then reduce oven to 350°F or Mark 4 and bake for further 20 to 30 minutes or until the pastry is golden brown. Serve with boiled potatoes and green peas. Serves 4 to 6.

METRIC CONVERSIONS

The weights, measures and oven temperatures used in the preceding recipes can be easily converted to their metric equivalents.

Weights

Avoirdupois	Metric
1 oz.	just under 30 grams
4 oz. (¼ lb.)	app. 115 grams
8 oz. (½ lb.)	app. 230 grams
1 lb.	454 grams

Liquid Measures

Imperial	Metric
1 tablespoon (liquid only)	20 millilitres
1 fl. oz.	app. 30 millilitres
1 gill (¼ pt.)	app. 145 millilitres
½ pt.	app. 285 millilitres
1 pt.	app. 570 millilitres
1 qt.	app. 1.140 litres

Oven Temperatures

	°Fahrenheit	Gas Mark	°Celsius
Slow	300	2	140
	325	3	158
Moderate	350	4	177
	375	5	190
	400	6	204
Hot	425	7	214
	450	8	232
	500	9	260

Flour as specified in these recipes refers to Plain Flour unless otherwise described.